DO I HAVE A DADDY?

Library of Congress Cataloging-in-Publication Data

Lindsay, Jeanne Warren.
    Do I have a daddy? : a story about a single-parent child with a
special section for single mothers and fathers / written by Jeanne
Warren Lindsay; illustrated by Cheryl Boeller. -- 2nd ed.
        48 p.
    Summary: A single mother explains to her son that his daddy left
soon after he was born. Includes section with suggestions for answer-
ing the question, "Do I have a daddy?"
    ISBN 0-930934-45-8 ;   -- ISBN 0-930934-44-x (pbk.) :
    1. Children of single parents--Psychology--Juvenile literature.
2. Paternal deprivation--Juvenile literature. [1. Single-parent family.
2. Unmarried mothers.] I. Boeller, Cheryl, 1953- ill. II. Title
Hq777.4.L56 1991
306.85'6--dc20
                                                    90-49676
                                                       CIP
                                                       AC

MORNING GLORY PRESS
6595 San Haroldo Way   Buena Park, CA 90620
                    714/828-1998
            Printed in the United States of America

DO I HAVE A DADDY?

A Story About a Single-Parent Child

With a Special Section for Single Mothers and Fathers

Written by Jeanne Warren Lindsay

Illustrated by Cheryl Boeller

Morning Glory Press

Buena Park, California

Erik and Jennifer were playing house.

"I'll cook the carrots while you sweep the floor," said Erik.

They were having fun . . . until Erik dropped the pan. It landed on Jennifer's foot.

"Ouch! That hurt!" she cried.

"That little pan couldn't hurt your foot," Erik said.

This made Jennifer mad.

"I'm going to tell my daddy," she said.

"Then I'll tell my daddy, too," replied Erik.

"But you don't have a daddy," said Jennifer.

"I do, too," said Erik.

"Where is he?" asked Jennifer.

"I . . . I don't know," said Erik.

Then he decided to go home.

"I was fixing carrots . . . but the pan dropped on Jennifer's foot and she got mad," Erik said to his mother.

"Poor Jennifer. I'll bet that hurt," said his mother.

"She's a big baby. I don't like her," Erik replied.

Suddenly Erik started crying.

"Where's my daddy?" he asked. "Do I have a daddy? Jennifer says I don't have a daddy."

"I'll tell you about your daddy," Mother said. "You had a daddy in the beginning. It takes both a mommy and a daddy to make a baby."

"But Jennifer's daddy lives with her," said Erik. "I've never seen my daddy."

"Lots of daddies and mommies like each other so much they get married," his mother explained.

"They live together and take care of their children together. That's what happened with Jennifer's mommy and daddy.

"Your daddy and I never lived together. We were very young when you were born. We weren't ready to get married. But I wanted you very much. I was so happy to have you."

"What about daddy? Didn't he want me?" asked Erik.

"Your daddy was excited. He came to see you when you were very little. But then he went away."

"Did he like me?" asked Erik.

"Oh yes! and he was very proud of you," Mother replied.

"Then why did he go away?" asked Erik.

"Caring for a baby is a big job," said Mother. "Your daddy wasn't ready for that."

"Oh," said Erik.

"If Jennifer says you don't have a daddy again, just tell her you had a daddy, but he's gone now," suggested Mother.

"OK," said Erik.

"You can help me put supper on the table," his mother told him.

A few days later Erik asked, "Will my daddy come back?"

"I don't think so," his mother answered.

"But I want a daddy like Jennifer's," Erik said.

"Perhaps you will someday," said his mother.

"You see, there are different kinds of daddies. Sometimes a daddy goes away as yours did. He may not see his children at all. Other daddies live with their children and help take care of them—like Jennifer's daddy.

"You might have a different daddy someday. If I get married, the man I marry will be your daddy, too."

"Are you getting married?" asked Erik.

"Not now," his mother replied. "But perhaps I will someday.

"For now, maybe you'd like to spend more time with Uncle Bob—and you know Grandpa plays with you and loves you."

"Maybe Grandpa would like to go for a walk with me now," said Erik.

Erik and his mother went into the living room.

"Will you go for a walk with me, Grandpa?" asked Erik.

"Sure, Erik. That's a good idea," Grandpa answered.

Special Section for Single Parents

Today many children are being reared by single parents. At least half the children in the United States will spend part of their growing-up years in a one-parent home.

If your child's father isn't around, how do you explain his absence? What do you tell him when he asks, "Where's Daddy?"

Divorced Parents

Lots of single-parent homes are the result of divorce. Children in these homes lived with both parents for awhile, then had to adjust to the changes caused by divorce.

In divorce, custody may be granted to the mother or to the father. The child lives most of the time with the parent who has custody, but may visit the other parent regularly.

Some divorced parents have joint custody of their child. They take turns parenting. Their child may live with her mother part of the time. At other times, she lives with her father. Their child is constantly reminded that both her mommy and daddy love her. Her parents can't live together any longer, but both want to be with her.

The child of divorced parents may have trouble accepting the break-up of her family. A child generally wants to live with both parents. If she can't, but she continues to have a good relationship with both, she can be reassured. She will know that they continue to care about her and that both parents love her.

Never-Married Parents

But what do you tell the child who doesn't know his daddy? What if his parents were never married? What if his father left before he was born? Or never even knew about his child?

Each year more than one out of six children born in the United States is born to a single mother. About two out of three teenage mothers who give birth are not married. Some of these single mothers have a close relationship with their baby's father. Some couples will eventually marry.

Sometimes, of course, a child's parents never marry each other. I've worked with more than 1200 pregnant teenagers in the past eighteen years. About half of these young women married their baby's father. Many of them were divorced within a short time.

The choice to remain single, although pregnant, is often a good decision for very young parents, according to many of my students. They point out that pregnancy alone is not a good enough reason to get married.

For some young mothers, marriage is not an option. The baby's father may be sure he isn't ready to get married. For some, learning about a girlfriend's pregnancy is scary.

Occasionally a young man refuses to admit he's going to be a father. "It isn't mine," he insists. Or he may leave town when he learns of the pregnancy.

Some women, whatever their age, deliberately choose to become single mothers. They want the satisfactions of motherhood but they don't wish to be married.

If his father isn't around, a child may indeed wonder, "Do I have a daddy?" This book may help answer that question.

Some children are reared by single fathers. For them, the question is, "Where's Mommy?" Because the vast majority of single-parent homes are headed by mothers, this book focuses on the child with an absent father. Suggestions for dealing with questions about a missing father, however, also apply to questions about an absent mother.

Before writing *Do I Have a Daddy?* I talked with many young mothers who didn't marry their baby's father. "How will you tell your child about his father?" I asked.

The first person I interviewed was Holly, mother of eighteen-month-old Orlando. Orlando's father, although still in town, had nothing to do with Holly since her third month of pregnancy. As far as Holly knows, he has never seen Orlando.

"I don't know what I'll tell him," Holly said. *"I've thought about it, but I don't have an answer. Please write your book soon so I'll know what to say!"*

Do I Have a Daddy? is a simple story. Erik's mother tells him his daddy saw him soon after he was born, but that he went away and probably won't be back. You can change this part of the story to fit your child's situation. It is best, however, to keep it as simple as possible while your child is very young.

Honesty Is Essential

In the story, Erik's mother attempts to be honest and positive about her child's father. She could have painted a negative picture of the man who couldn't face his parenthood responsibilities. Or she could have lied to Erik. She might have found it easier to say his daddy was a wonderful person, and that he died. But she knows how important it is to be honest with her child.

Saying "He made a mistake, and he let us down" is not a terrible thing to say—if that's how it was. If you and your child's father loved each other at the time you conceived, share that fact with your child. But be honest.

Most of the young mothers stressed the need for honesty. They generally wanted their children to feel good about their fathers, but they also knew they shouldn't fake it.

A lady I work with said she never told her little boy about his dad. He's about nine now, and he's getting upset with her. He's having a lot of problems. He says, "I think you're lying to me—I don't think I even have a father." (Alison, 19, mother of Stevie, 15 months)

I don't plan on telling Karl things that were bad about Bob. After all, he is Karl's father. But if Karl asks me point-blank why I left him, I'll tell him. I'll tell him Bob has a violent temper and we couldn't cope with that.

My mother never did tell me why my dad left, but my grandma finally did. She said he hit my mom so she left him.

My mom still won't talk about it. She just says they were too young to get married, and that it didn't work out.

I resent the fact that she didn't tell me. I don't like the idea that he hit my mother, but he is still my dad. (Kimberly, 18—Karl, 15 months)

Stress Positive Points

Rita Blau, psychologist, feels it is very important for a child to have contact with both parents if possible. If that can't happen, she advises, it's best to try to find some good things about the father. "I think it's important to let the baby know, no matter how you feel, that there was something good about this man. Your child is part of both parents. If one parent is all bad, she may think she is bad, too," she said. Robin, Erin, and Jill agree:

Why make a kid feel like his father was a louse? If his dad's a louse, that makes him half-louse. It's not fair to lay your feelings on your child.

I tell Stu, "Your father wasn't as lucky as I am—he didn't get to live with you." (Robin, 21—Stu, 5 years)

I wouldn't want to tell Meghan, "Your dad wasn't good for anything, he couldn't do anything." I want to tell her the good things about him. I'll tell her he was a hard worker, and that he liked sports. We had a lot of good times and a lot of bad times—but I don't want to think

back to the bad times. I'll tell her how it was before, that we enjoyed ourselves together, and how he left.

I feel now that maybe he wasn't ready to take on the responsibility. Perhaps he thought, "I have too many things ahead of me to settle down now with a family." (Erin, 17—Meghan, 10 months)

What will I tell him? That's a hard question. I'll probably say, "Well, we both really loved each other but we were real young at the time. He wasn't ready to be a father." I believe if we had been older, we probably would have gotten married.

I would never tell him his father is no good. I want Todd to know Sal is a good person. Sometimes I have bad feelings about him, but I don't think I'll share those with Todd. (Jill, 19—Todd, 3 years)

Totally-Absent Father

Sometimes a pregnancy occurs between two people who don't have a lasting relationship at all. Occasionally, a mother may not know much about her baby's father—or she may not be quite sure who he was. What can she tell her child? How can she be honest, yet not unduly hurtful?

Maria's parents didn't let her date. She resented this. When she was 16, she ran away for a few days, then returned home. By the time she learned—to her horror—that she was pregnant, she had completely lost contact with her baby's father.

He never knew he had a child, and Maria's parents never learned the identity of their grandson's father.

When Pedro was about a year old, Maria explained:

I'm going to tell him about his father . . . No, he wasn't good at all, and I'm not going to tell Pedro a lie. He was so bad that I was even thinking of telling Pedro later that his father died.

He was nothing to be proud of. I was real young, and I didn't know anything then. But I'm going to tell Pedro what happened. I don't want him to do the same thing—that was a bad mistake. (Maria, 18—Pedro, 1 year)

Maria might say, "Pedro, your father and I weren't close. We didn't plan to have a baby together. In fact, your father never even knew I was pregnant. I thought it was best both for you and for me not to tell him."

Then Maria might add, "But I'm very glad I have you and I love you very much. I'm sure your daddy would love you a lot, too, if he could know you."

Later, if Pedro asks more questions, Maria may be willing to give him more information. If she knows almost nothing about Pedro's father, she may simply level with him. If she feels okay about the situation, Pedro will probably feel okay, too.

Importance of Feeling OK

That's the secret, feeling all right about your life and your child's life, according to psychologist Jean Bayard, Santa Clara, California, Counseling Center.

"Of course what you tell your child about his father is important, but even more important is how *you* feel about the situation," said Dr. Bayard. "Your child will pick up from you the OK-ness or not-OK-ness of being a single parent and of not knowing one's father."

"I know you wish you had a daddy who lives with us. That would be very nice. Right now, though, we have each other."

If you feel you're doing all right as a single parent, and you take it for granted that your parenting will go well, your child is likely to pick up that same feeling. After all, there's no natural law that says a child must live with and be brought up by a father, any more than he should be in contact with a grandparent or with aunts and uncles, explained Dr. Bayard.

On the other hand, if you feel sorry for your child because his daddy is not around, your child may pick up the idea that he is to be pitied. He may then feel resentful and unsure about his ability to cope without his father.

Your child's feelings are important, too. If he seems upset when you talk with him about his father, encourage him to share those feelings. You might say, "I know you wish you had a daddy who lives with us. That would be very nice. Right now, though, we have each other."

A child with an absent parent may develop a fantasy about that parent, such as "My father is a prince who will take me away." This is normal, according to licensed therapist Eugenie Wheeler, Ventura, California. If your situation seems more complicated, however, Ms. Wheeler recommends professional counseling.

It's important that both you and your child understand that a family can be any group of people who care about each other. It doesn't have to be the traditional family with a mother, father, and child. A family can be a mother and child, a father and child, grandparent and child, or other grouping. These can all be "normal" families.

If you have an only child and you are an only parent, you will want to make a special effort for your child to be with other kids. When you take your son or daughter for an outing, for example, take another child along.

Your Own Feelings

The importance of examining your own feelings is also stressed by Catherine Monserrat, Ph. D., former counselor at New Futures School, Albuquerque, New Mexico.

"How did you feel when your child's father left?" she asks.

"Sometimes you may see a resemblance between your child and his father," Dr. Monserrat continued. "You may be tempted to let your frustrations with his father spill over on your child. It's important for you to recognize this possibility.

"Don't transfer those frustrations to your child. He's not just 'David's son.' Instead, your son is Bruce, and Bruce is a person. He is not an extension of David. Don't expect him either to act like or not to act like his father. Expect him to be himself," Dr. Monserrat advises.

Sometimes people attempt to preserve the father through the child. To avoid doing this, you may need to work through feelings of rejection and abandonment. Examine those feelings. What were your expectations in your relationship with your child's father? In what ways were you disappointed by him? How did he let you down? It may take time to get over your disappointment and anger. Start by understanding that your feelings are important.

If you feel resentful about being a single parent and you aren't sure you can make it, get counseling, advises Ms. Wheeler.

"If you feel your depression is going on too long or if your child appears too troubled, call your local mental health agency for help. Or ask your school counselor where you could get assistance," she suggests.

Remember that to fulfill your child's needs, you must also meet your own needs. You really can't give your child good care unless you also take care of yourself. So be aware of your own needs, and work out ways of meeting those needs as well as caring for your child. If there is no co-parent, it's especially important that there be some kind of adult feedback for you, Ms. Wheeler stressed.

Your child needs the companionship of other children—and you need the companionship of other adults. Perhaps you will want to contact the local Parents Without Partners organization or some other group of single parents.

Male Role Model

If your father or your brother is around, encourage him to spend time with your child. Having a male role model is helpful for a child who doesn't know his father.

They play with my male friends. They call them Uncle Skip and Uncle Bob. (Leslie, 21—Amy, 3 years, and Kerry, 16 months)

In your eagerness to provide a father figure, however, you may want every date to fill that role. The danger here is that your child may form an attachment with each man in your life, an attachment that may have to be broken.

Instead, encourage your child to enjoy your male friends as his friends, too. Don't suggest he call each one "Daddy"—unless and until you feel your relationship with the man is truly long-term.

"Right" Time to Talk

When do you tell a child about her father? Do you wait until she's old enough to understand everything? Or do you answer questions as they're asked?

It's usually better to answer questions whenever your child asks them. If a 3-year-old asks about her daddy, you will probably answer her much more simply than you will if a 6-year-old asks the same question. But it is important that you answer her. Don't say, "We'll talk about that when you're older." She may not ask again.

John hasn't asked about his biological father yet, but I'm prepared to answer any questions he may have. I want to help him understand why we never married. I've put away two pictures of his father in case John wants to know what he looked like. I also saved cards and letters he gave me years ago. I thought it would be better to save these things for John.

I never was told much about my real father, and my mother tried to poison my mind when she did tell me about him. I don't want John ever to think I was doing the same thing. The letters I saved will tell him more about his father than I ever could. (Ronda, 21—John, 4 years)

What I tell them depends on their questions. So far, they aren't asking. The little boy next door has a father—and Amy realizes that's Mike's daddy. But she doesn't think more about it. She knows she doesn't have one.

When they start asking questions, I'll tell them it would never have worked out. We would have had more problems with their father than we have without him.

They're not worried about a father now. They realize it's just them and me. I guess it's if you have someone around at the beginning that you miss him later. (Susan)

A research study in England supports Susan's viewpoint. The National Child Development Study traced the development of 17,000 children, and a report dealing with one-parent families in the study was published. The children of widowed and never-married mothers were compared with those whose parents were separated or divorced.

Having separated or divorced parents seemed to add more problems to the children's lives than did either having a widowed or a never-married parent. The researchers suggested that continuing tension between divorced or separated parents can affect the children even after the final split.

Another part of the explanation may be that children tend to accept "what is." They may find it harder to understand and accept the fact that parents who lived together for awhile *actually chose* to separate or divorce.

Risks of Cover-Up

If you marry someone else when your child is very young, you may think it easier not to mention that your child's step or adoptive father is not his biological father. After all, you may ask, what is a "real" father?

Her biological father isn't her only real daddy. If her stepfather treats her as a "real" dad would, then he's a "real" father. (Erin)

Erin, of course, is right. Fathering goes far beyond the biological fact of conception. In fact, the term "real father" seems to fit best the man who "acts like" a father.

What is a father? I think a father is a 24-hour person— someone who is there. He's there not just to say "Hi" and "Goodbye," but to teach his child. It's a little more than supporting a child, too. I guess it's sort of like spreading yourself into the kid. (Jill)

A step-father, adoptive father, or foster father may do a lot of "spreading himself into the kid" while the child may never know his biological father. So why should you even mention his first father?

In fact, your child's "real" (acting) father may have trouble with his own feelings in this matter. He may want very much to ignore the fact that he is not your child's biological father.

Eric gets jealous if I mention Heidi's father. But some day I will probably tell Heidi most of the story. It may have to be behind Eric's back, but Heidi needs to know what happened. It's something I have to do myself.

If my mom were in this situation, I would want to know. I think it's only fair to be honest with Heidi. (Jenny, 19—Heidi, 2 years)

Ignoring the reality of the biological father is likely to backfire. If you don't tell him, the risk is great that your child will someday hear about his "other" father from someone else. He may be quite young when this happens. Or he may not hear it until he is grown.

Whenever it happens, however, the knowledge that his parents kept such important information from him is likely to hurt a lot.

I do think you have got to be honest about it. Some people get married to someone else and act like he is the real father. But kids find out somehow. (Jill)

Hiding information usually makes that information, once it is discovered, seem much worse. Think about it. If you had always assumed one person was your father—but today you learn that he isn't—how will you react?

Most of us would be quite resentful and would think our parents lied to us.

Now consider yourself in another situation. You have been brought up by two loving parents. You have always known you had another father in the beginning, but he has never been a part of your life. Would you still feel so resentful?

Most of us, I think, would feel much better about the latter situation. If our parents love us and care about us, we can generally accept them as the human beings they are. But if they lie to us, we lose our trust in them.

Sandy married Carl a few months after Seth was born. Carl is not Seth's biological father. Sandy asked, "Should Carl be with me when I tell Seth about his biological father? Or should I tell him by myself?"

The answer depends on Sandy's and Carl's feelings. If Carl feels threatened, perhaps he shouldn't be involved. But if he is close to Seth, he may want to share this part of parenting, too. If Carl can handle it, Seth may feel better if he is included.

If Daddy Returns

Erin brought up another question:

I haven't figured out what to tell Meghan when she wants to see her father. He lives in another state, but he might come back one day. What should I tell her?

As long as Meghan's father lives elsewhere, Erin can simply say, "No, you can't see your father because he doesn't live here." If he comes back, the answer is not so simple.

He may have a legal right to see his daughter. Unless her stepfather adopts Meghan, Patrick will still be her legal father. Erin may be required by the court to let him spend time with Meghan.

As a single mother—or if you are married to someone other than your child's legal father—you need to be aware of the father's rights. If he is paying child support, what are his rights? If he isn't providing any support, does he have any rights?

Does it make any difference whether or not your child has his last name?

The father who pays child support generally has a right to see his child. Even if he provides no support, he may still have that right. Whether or not your child has his father's last name may not make much difference in the rights his father has.

However, answers to these questions vary from state to state. Check with a lawyer or with your local legal aid office.

If your husband would like to adopt your child, you need to know about fathers' rights in adoption in your state. Contact an adoption agency for this information.

You may have a choice as to whether or not your child's father sees her. If you do, think first about what is best for your child. Sometimes mothers have trouble with their own feelings on this issue.

Keeping a child away from her father in order to spite the father is not good for the child. Neither is insisting that she spend time with her father if neither of them wants a relationship.

The best interests of your child must be the deciding factor. If she sees her father, she should feel good about it.

Use of This Book

Do I Have a Daddy? can be used in several ways. First, it may be read to a child whose life story is similar to Erik's. Hearing Erik's story may help the child start to talk about his own problems. If most of his friends have two parents, he knows he is different. He needs to be able to talk to an adult about his feelings about not knowing his father.

The story may also be read to children in different situations including those who live with their fathers and mothers. It may help these children understand and accept life styles different from their own.

Other Books by Jeanne Warren Lindsay

TEENS PARENTING, Book One:
The Pregnancy and Newborn Challenge
By Jeanne Lindsay and Jean Brunelli
Book Two: The Baby and Toddler Challenge
By Jeanne Warren Lindsay
Book Three: The Discipline Challenge
By Jeanne Lindsay and Sally McCullough
Child development/parenting books written especially
for school-age parents. **Contact MGP for information.
(First edition, a single book, is listed on order blank.)**

TEEN PREGNANCY CHALLENGE, BOOK 1: Strategies for Change
TEEN PREGNANCY CHALLENGE, BOOK 2: Programs for Kids
By Jeanne Lindsay and Sharon Rodine
Two books to help you develop/expand adolescent pregnancy prevention and care programs. Real hands-on
guidance. Includes the nuts and bolts of implementing
and managing a teen pregnancy prevention and care
program.
256 pp. ea. Paper, $12.95 ea., set, $24.95;
Cloth, $19.95 ea., $34.95/set

TEENAGE MARRIAGE:
Coping with Reality
Gives teens a picture of the realities of marriage—a look
at the difficulties they may encounter if they say "I do"
. . . or simply move in together . . . too soon.
208 pp. Paper, $9.95 Cloth, $15.95   Study Guide, $2.50
Teacher's Guide (for both marriage books) $5.95

TEENS LOOK AT MARRIAGE:
Rainbows, Roles and Reality
Readable *interesting* discussion of research behind
Teenage Marriage. Includes a wealth of statistical
information about teenagers' attitudes toward marriage
and living together.
256 pp. Paper, $9.95 Cloth, $15.95 Study Guide, $2.50

SCHOOL-AGE PARENTS:
The Challenge of Three-Generation Living
Families experiencing the drama of three-generation
living—parents, teenage daughter, and her child—share
their pain, their confusion, and their anguish—and
positive solutions. Excellent guidance for families
struggling with three-generation living.
224 pp. Paper, $10.95; Cloth, $17.95

Books on Adoption

PREGNANT TOO SOON:
Adoption Is an Option
For teens. True personal stories together with the latest
information on agency and independent adoption, fathers'
rights, dealing with grief, and other aspects of adoption.
224 pp. Paper, $9.95

PARENTS, PREGNANT TEENS AND THE ADOPTION OPTION: Help for Families
For birthgrandparents—those who lose a grandchild to
adoption. Helps parents cope with shock of daughter's
too-early pregnancy and deal with the inevitable grieving
they and their daughter will experience after placement.
208 pp. Paper, $8.95; Cloth, $11.95

ADOPTION AWARENESS: A Guide for Teachers, Counselors, Nurses, Caring Others
By Jeanne Lindsay and Catherine Monserrat
For you—if you ever help pregnant women and their
partners make informed decisions about their own and
their babies' futures. Extremely sensitive to needs of
all those in the adoption triangle, especially birthparents.
288 pp. Paper, $12.95; Cloth, $17.95

OPEN ADOPTION: A Caring Option
Describes new world of adoption in which birthparents
and adoptive parents may continue contact after adoption
is finalized. Many quotes. 256 pp. Pap., $9.95; Cloth, $15.95

MAIL ORDER FORM   # Morning Glory Press

6595–A San Haroldo Way / Buena Park, CA 90620–3748 / (714) 828–1998 / FAX (714) 828–2049

Please send me the following:

QUANTITY	TITLE	BULK ORDER DISCOUNT (IF ANY)	UNIT PRICE	TOTAL PRICE
SCHOOL-AGE PARENTS—THREE-GENERATION LIVING				
	Quality Paper. ISBN 0–930934–36–9	10/$100	10.95	
	Hardcover. ISBN 0–930934–37–7	10/$160	17.95	
TEEN PREGNANCY CHALLENGE: BOOK 1 - STRATEGIES FOR CHANGE				
	Quality Paper. ISBN 0–930934–34–2		14.95	
	Hardcover. ISBN 0–930934–35–0		19.95	
TEEN PREGNANCY CHALLENGE: BOOK 2 - PROGRAMS FOR KIDS				
	Quality Paper. ISBN 0–930934–38–5		14.95	
	Hardcover. ISBN 0–930934–39–3		19.95	
—COMBINATION SPECIAL— TEEN PREGNANCY CHALLENGE: BOOKS 1 & 2				
	Quality Paper. ISBN 0–930934–40–7		24.95	
	Hardcover. ISBN 0–930934–41–5		34.95	
TEENAGE MARRIAGE				
	Quality Paper. ISBN 0–930934–30–x	5/$45; 10/$80; 25/$175	9.95	
	Hardcover. ISBN 0–930934–31–8	5/$75; 10/$135; 25/$325	15.95	
	Student Guide. ISBN 0–930934–13–x	10/$20; 25/$40	2.50	
	Teacher's Guide*. ISBN 0–930934–19–9 *Includes Teacher's Guide for **Teens Look at Marriage**		5.95	
TEENS LOOK AT MARRIAGE				
	Quality Paper. ISBN 0–930934–15–6	5/$45; 10/$80; 25/$175	9.95	
	Hardcover. ISBN 0–930934–16–4	5/$75; 10/$135; 25/$325	15.95	
	Study Guide. ISBN 0–930934–20–2	10/$20; 25/$40	2.50	
TEENAGE PREGNANCY				
	Spiral Bound, Paper. ISBN 0–945886–00–4	10/$95; 25/$225	10.00	
	Study Guide (Consumable)		2.00	
TEENS PARENTING — First Edition				
	Quality Paper. ISBN 0–930934–06–7	5/$45; 10/$80; 25/$175	9.95	
	Student Guide. ISBN 0–930934–08–3	10/$20; 25/$40	2.50	
	Teacher's Guide. ISBN 0–930934–09–1		5.95	
WORKING WITH CHILDBEARING ADOLESCENTS				
	Spiral Bound, Paper.		12.95	
DO I HAVE A DADDY?				
	Quality Paper, ISBN 0-930934-44-x		5.95	
	Hardcover, ISBN 0-930934-45-8		12.95	
SAY "NO!" TO VIOLENCE				
	Quality Paper.		6.00	
	One FREE Study Guide		N/C	
SUB-TOTAL of Column One Carry over to Column Two where marked with ★				

QUANTITY	TITLE	BULK ORDER DISCOUNT (IF ANY)	UNIT PRICE	TOTAL PRICE
ADOPTION AWARENESS				
	Quality Paper. ISBN 0–930934–32–6	5/$60; 10/$115	12.95	
	Hardcover. ISBN 0–930934–33–4	5/$85; 10/$160	17.95	
OPEN ADOPTION: A CARING OPTION				
	Quality Paper. ISBN 0–930934–23–7	5/$45; 10/$80; 25/$175	9.95	
	Hardcover. ISBN 0–930934–22–9	5/$75; 10/$135; 25/$325	15.95	
	Study/Discussion Guide AND Teacher's Guide. ISBN 0–930934–24–5		2.00	
	Additional copies of Study Guide		.50	
PARENTS, PREGNANT TEENS AND THE ADOPTION OPTION				
	Quality Paper. ISBN 0–930934–28–8	10/$80	8.95	
	Hardcover. ISBN 0–930934–29–6 (no dust jacket)		11.95	
PREGNANT TOO SOON				
	Quality Paper. ISBN 0–930934–25–3	5/$45; 10/$80; 25/$175	9.95	
	Study/Discussion Guide AND Teacher's Guide. ISBN 0–930934–27–x		2.00	
	Additional copies of Study Guide		.50	
TO KEERA WITH LOVE				
	Quality Paper. ISBN 1–55612–072–9		8.95	
	Study/Discussion Guide	10+/.50 ea.	1.00	
PAMPHLET: "You Can Help: Curriculum Guide"				
	16 pp. Single Copy FREE!	10/$7.50	1.00	

SUB-TOTAL — Column Two

ADD Sub-Total from Column One ★

TOTAL — Both Columns

Please add postage: 1–3 books, $2.00; 4 or more, .60 per book. Maximum shipping: $12.50. (Shipments outside U.S. require additional postage)

California residents add 6.25% sales tax.

TOTAL ENCLOSED

Advance payment in U.S. funds required on all orders shipped outside the United States. School/Library Purchase Orders accepted. If not satisfied, return in 15 days for refund.

Name _____

Address _____

City / State / Zip _____